Contents

Spotlight On My Country

Created by Bobbie Kalman

For Allan MacKay, who lived in Kenya and loved it,
with thanks for your help with this book

**Author and
Editor-in-Chief**
Bobbie Kalman

Editor
Kathy Middleton

Proofreader
Crystal Sikkens

Research
Marcella Haanstra

Photo research
Bobbie Kalman

Design
Bobbie Kalman
Katherine Berti
Samantha Crabtree (cover)

Print and production coordinator
Katherine Berti

Photographs
Digital Vision: page 29 (bl)
Shutterstock: back cover, pages 4, 5, 9, 10, 11, 18 (t, bm),
    18–19 (background), 19 (b), 21, 22 (b), 23 (m), 24–25
    (background), 26 (b), 27 (ml, b, tr), 29 (t, br), 30 (b),
    31 (tr); Pichugin Dmitry: front cover (woman); Anna
    Omelchenko: front cover (background); pages 3, 6, 14,
    15 (t); lexan: page 7 (br); spirit of america: pages 13 (tr,
    bl), 17 (bl), 25 (b); Denis Kuvaev: page 13 (br); africa924:
    pages 16, 17 (br), 22 (t); meunierd: page 17 (tl); Arnold
    John Labrentz: page 17 (tr); testing: page 19 (t);
    Stanislaw Tokarski: pages 20, 23 (t); Sadik Gulec: page
    24 (b); urosr: page 25 (t); Vadim Petrakov: page 31 (b)
Thinkstock: pages 1, 8, 12 (t), 13 (tl), 18 (bl, br), 23 (b),
    26 (t), 27 (tl), 28 (b), 30 (t), 31 (tl)
Wikimedia Commons: Xavigivax: page 7 (bl); Angela
    Sevin: page 12 (b); Doron: page 15 (b)

t=top, b=bottom, m=middle, tl=top left, tr=top right,
bl=bottom left, br=bottom right, bm=bottom middle,
ml=middle left

Library and Archives Canada Cataloguing in Publication

Kalman, Bobbie
     Spotlight on Kenya / Bobbie Kalman.

(Spotlight on my country)
Includes index.
Issued also in electronic format.
ISBN 978-0-7787-0866-7 (bound).--ISBN 978-0-7787-0870-4 (pbk.)

     1. Kenya--Juvenile literature. I. Title. II. Series: Spotlight on
my country

DT433.522.K35 2013   j967.62   C2013-900669-9

Library of Congress Cataloging-in-Publication Data

Kalman, Bobbie.
     Spotlight on Kenya / Bobbie Kalman.
          pages cm. -- (Spotlight on my country)
     Includes index.
     ISBN 978-0-7787-0866-7 (reinforced library binding)
-- ISBN 978-0-7787-0870-4 (pbk.) -- ISBN 978-1-4271-9297-4
(electronic pdf) -- ISBN 978-1-4271-9221-9 (electronic html)
     1. Kenya--Juvenile literature. I. Title. II. Series: Spotlight on my country.

     DT433.522.K36 2013
     967.62--dc23

                                                  2013003286

Crabtree Publishing Company

Printed in Canada/092018/MQ20180817

www.crabtreebooks.com   1-800-387-7650

Published in Canada
Crabtree Publishing
616 Welland Ave.
St. Catharines, Ontario
L2M 5V6

Published in the United States
Crabtree Publishing
PMB 59051
350 Fifth Avenue, 59th Floor
New York, New York 10118

Published in the United Kingdom
Crabtree Publishing
Maritime House
Basin Road North, Hove
BN41 1WR

Published in Australia
Crabtree Publishing
3 Charles Street
Coburg North
VIC 3058

Seven continents and five oceans

Kenya is part of the **continent** of Africa. A continent is a huge area of land. The seven continents, from largest to smallest, are Asia, Africa, North America, South America, Antarctica, Europe, and Australia/Oceania. Kenya is a **tropical** country, which means it is close to the **equator**. The equator is an imaginary line around the center of Earth. Countries that are close to the equator have hotter weather than those that are farther away.

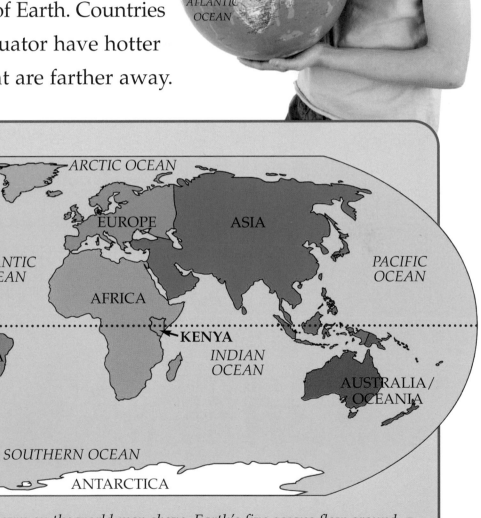

The seven continents are shown on the world map above. Earth's five oceans flow around the continents. What are the names of the five oceans? Which ocean touches Kenya?

Welcome to Kenya!

Kenya is a fascinating country with beautiful landscapes, amazing animals, and a very long history. Kenya was once a **colony** of Britain. In 1963, it became **independent**, or free from Britain's control. The country is now called the **Republic** of Kenya. A republic is not ruled by a king or queen. People vote for the leader of their country. In Kenya, the president is the head of the country and of the government. A vice president is second in command. A prime minister helps with government business.

The two official languages of Kenya are English and Swahili. Hello in Swahili is Jambo, *and goodbye is* Kwa heri!

Kenya's flag has three main colors—with a white line around the red stripe. The black stands for the heritage of most of Kenya's people, the red symbolizes Kenya's struggle for independence, the white stands for peace, and the green stands for the country's agriculture. In the center of the flag there is a large warrior shield and two spears. The shield represents Kenya's determination to defend its freedom.

HARAMBEE

The coat of arms of Kenya features two lions holding spears and a shield. The lion is the national symbol of Kenya. The shield and spears show that people will fight to defend their freedom. The country's motto is "Harambee," which means **unity**, or "pulling together." The rooster holding an ax shows power, success, and the willingness to work. The rooster is moving forward, which stands for the start of a new day.

Nairobi is the capital of Kenya. About 3.1 million people live in this city. Nairobi has both modern skyscrapers and poor, rundown areas (see page 22).

Kenya's landforms

Landforms are different shapes of land. Some of Kenya's landforms include vast grasslands called **savannas**, unspoiled beaches, tropical forests, high snow-capped mountains, deep **canyons**, volcanoes, hot, dry deserts, and cool **highlands**, or hilly areas. Kenya is famous for its Great Rift **Valley**, also called the East African Rift, which runs from the north of the country to its south. A valley is a low area of land between mountains or hills. The Great Rift Valley has some shallow lakes, such as Lake Victoria, Lake Bogoria, and Lake Nakuru, shown on the opposite page.

*Mount Kenya is Kenya's highest mountain. It is one of more than 27 **volcanoes** in Kenya. A volcano is a mountain made from **lava** that has cooled after shooting out of Earth's crust. Mount Kenya is no longer an active volcano. Even though it is close to the equator, Mount Kenya has snow at its peak.*

Lake Nakuru is famous for the brilliant pink flamingos that flock there by the thousands. The lake is part of the Great Rift Valley.

Kenya's Great Rift Valley is so big that it can be seen from space!

The coast of Kenya

Kenya has 333 miles (536 km) of **coast** along the Indian Ocean. A coast is where ocean touches land. There are long stretches of sandy beaches with palm trees growing along the shores. Many kinds of monkeys, butterflies, and birds live along the coast. Tourists travel to Kenya to swim in the beautiful **coral reefs**. Coral reefs are made by tiny animals called **coral polyps**. When coral polyps die, the coverings on their bodies pile up and form coral reefs. Many kinds of fish, such as the dragon moray eel on page 11, live in coral reefs.

The most beautiful beaches in Africa are along the Indian Ocean in Kenya. The weather is hot all year because the beaches are near the equator. This Maasai man enjoys a view of the ocean.

This dragon moray eel lives in a coral reef off the coast of Kenya. Moray eels are fish that are found in warm ocean waters. They hunt fish and other animals that live in oceans.

mangrove forest

beach

Kenya has several islands off its coast. This one is called Chale Island. Chale Island has beautiful beaches and coral reefs. The island is covered by a thick **mangrove** forest.

11

The people of Kenya

*Most Bantu people are farmers.
Some grow tea and coffee.*

*This woman belongs to the Kikuyu
group. She is wearing traditional
clothing and makeup.*

There are more than 41 million people living in Kenya. Most Kenyans are of African descent. They are identified within three main language groups: Bantu, Nilotic, and Afroasiatic. The rest of the population is made up of the descendants of European, Arabic, and Asian **settlers**.

The Bantu

Bantu speakers form the largest group. They came to Kenya about 2,000 years ago. They are farmers who produce most of Kenya's food. Many live on the land around Mount Kenya, but some **tribes**, or groups, have moved to the central part of the country. Hundreds of ethnic groups speak Bantu languages. The biggest group is the Kikuyu, who number about eight million people. Jomo Kenyatta, Kenya's first president after independence, was a Kikuyu.

These girls and their mother were born in Kenya. Their ancestors came to Kenya from England.

Wangari Muta Maathai, a Kikuyu, was the first African woman to receive the Nobel Peace Prize for promoting conservation and women's rights.

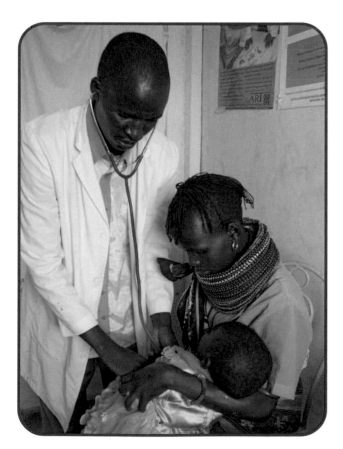

Today, there are more doctors in Kenya, and people are getting better health care. This doctor is giving a baby a checkup.

Many of the world's fastest runners come from an area above the Rift Valley. They train very hard to become the best runners in the world.

13

Maasai and Samburu

Maasai men perform a traditional dance called the ipid, *in which young warriors jump high into the air. This man is jumping very high! How high can you jump?*

The Maasai and Samburu people of Kenya belong to the Nilotic group. The Maasai are among the best-known native Kenyans. They are recognized for their colorful dress and customs. They live near the **game parks** of East Africa, where tourists from all over the world watch animals roam in their **habitats**, or natural homes.

New ways of life

Traditionally, the Maasai travel from place to place to feed their cattle, which they use as their food. Many Maasai, however, have moved away from their **nomadic** lives to work in the cities. Some work as security guards, waiters, and guides in tourist areas, such as the resorts along Mombasa Beach.

The Samburu

The Samburu are also part of the Nilotic group. They are related to the Maasai but are separate from them. They speak a similar language called Samburu.

Semi-nomadic

The Samburu live in the Rift Valley province of Northern Kenya. They are semi-nomadic and move every few weeks to find fresh plants on which their animals can feed. The Samburu usually live in groups of five to ten families. Men look after the animals and keep their tribes safe. Women take care of the homes, gather vegetables, look after the children, and collect water.

The Samburu today

Many Samburu do not want to settle in one area because it means changing their way of life. Some men, however, have taken jobs in the cities as security guards.

Samburu women keep their hair short and wear colorful beaded necklaces, earrings, and bracelets. Both men and women wear jewelry, which is made by the women.

The Samburu live north of the equator in Samburu District. Its landscape includes forests, savannas, and deserts.

15

Kenya's children

Children in Kenya can go to school for free, but many families need them to work. As a result, very few go on to high school or university. In some of the poorer areas of Kenya, a new type of school called a "harambee school" has developed. In this type of school, the government provides a teacher, and the community builds the schoolhouse. By working together this way, the children in a community can get an education.

The children in this community school are Maasai children. They wear purple and pink uniforms.

These young girls must walk through mud to get to school, but they are happy to go.

These children live in the country. The older ones help take care of the younger ones.

Many children like to play soccer and rugby. These boys are playing soccer at their school.

These young boys are learning martial arts in Malindi, Kenya. They are practicing judo.

What is culture?

Kenya has many **cultures**. Culture is the beliefs, customs, and ways of life that a group of people shares. Ways of life include the way people dress, the foods they eat, the crafts they make, and the sports and games they play. People also create art, music, and dances to **express**, or show, their cultures. Music is very important to the people of Kenya. They use music to pass down stories about daily life, wars, and family history. The images on these pages show how Kenyans express their cultures through art and music.

Both Maasai men and women wear colorful necklaces and other fancy jewelry. The color red stands for power.

Wood carving is a popular form of art in Kenya.

Bomas of Kenya is a cultural center near Nairobi National Park. Talented artists perform traditional dances and songs taken from the country's forty two different tribal groups.

Drums, shakers, and thumb pianos are used in Kenyan music.

drum

thumb piano

shakers

Life long ago

Some of the earliest humans on Earth may have lived in Kenya more than a million years ago. **Archaeologists**, or people who study human history, have found very old human bones buried there. Thousands of years ago, people from other parts of Africa, such as the Bantu people, moved to Kenya and are still there today. Arabic, Chinese, and Indian people sailed to Kenya's coast many years later, to trade goods. In 1498, a Portuguese explorer named Vasco da Gama reached the east coast of Africa. The Portuguese set up trading settlements and built Fort Jesus on the coast. Between 1696 and 1698, Arabic people from northern Africa drove out the Portuguese and took over the trading settlements.

*Fort Jesus is in Mombasa, Kenya. From the air, the fort looks like the shape of a person looking out at the ocean. Today, the fort houses a museum containing **artifacts** from Kenya's early history. Artifacts are historic objects made by people.*

Under British rule

In the 19th century, European countries such as Britain and Germany started claiming land in Africa. In 1895, Kenya became a British colony, and its people did not have a say about what happened in their country. The British built a railway from Nairobi to Kisumu, a city on Lake Victoria. When the railway was completed, British settlers came by the thousands to farm large areas of land. They became wealthy from farming coffee and tea, whereas most Kenyan farmers remained poor.

British soldier

Becoming independent

In 1952, the Mau Mau revolt took place. In that conflict, a group of Kikuyu Kenyans battled against the British from 1952 to 1960. Jomo Kenyatta was one of the leaders. Finally in 1963, Kenya became an independent country and a republic. Kenyatta became the first prime minister in 1963, then president in 1964. He is known as the founding father of the Kenyan nation.

*The shilling is the **currency**, or money, used in Kenya. Jomo Kenyatta's picture is on some of the bills.*

Kenya's cities

These children live in a poor area in Nairobi. They have difficult lives.

Nairobi is the capital of Kenya. The area where this city now stands was once a pasture for Maasai cattle. The Maasai named Nairobi after a river that they called *Enkare Nyrobi*, or "Cold Water." Nairobi began as a colonial railway station and grew into an important trading center by the twentieth century. When the railway was built, the area was cleared of trees. Later, trees had to be replanted to create shade for the city!

*Nairobi is a busy city with modern buildings and many trees along the streets. It also has crowded **slums**, or poor areas, where people live together in shacks.*

22

Mombasa

Mombasa is on the coast of Kenya. It is Kenya's second-largest city and main **port**. A port is a harbor where ships load and unload their goods. Mombasa was an important place for trade with India, China, northern Africa, and Portugal (see page 20).

Two huge sets of elephant tusks were built to honor the visit of Britain's Queen Elizabeth II to Mombasa in 1952. They are made out of aluminum.

Kenya's oldest town

The town of Lamu is on Lamu Island. People have lived there longer than in any other town in Kenya. The first people there were the Swahili, a Bantu group.

Almost a million people live in Mombasa. They come from many cultures. Above is a Jain temple built by people from India who live in Mombasa. It is the first Jain temple built outside India.

*Muslims make up most of the population of Lamu. There are more than 20 **mosques**, or Muslim places of worship. This mosque is on a beach on the Indian Ocean.*

Kenya's challenges

Kenya is facing many challenges today. Some of its people live in terrible conditions. The cities in Kenya have become overcrowded, as their populations have grown very quickly. Kenya also provides shelter to nearly a million **refugees** from nearby African countries. The refugees arrive from war-torn Somalia and Sudan and stay in special camps until it is safe for them to return home. There has also been a terrible **drought**, or long period without rain. There is not enough water for drinking or growing food, and many people are starving.

Dadaab is a town in the North Eastern Province in Kenya. It is the largest refugee camp in the world. Dadaab hosts people who have fled various conflicts in Eastern Africa. Most have come because of war in southern Somalia.

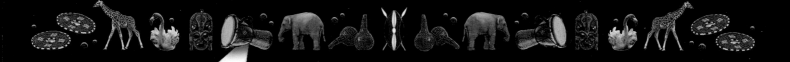

These women and children are getting water from a well outside their village, but some people have to walk long distances to find clean water.

More schools are being built in Kenya. With better education, children will have better lives.

Amazing wildlife!

Cheetahs live on the savanna. They are the fastest land animals on Earth.

Some of the most amazing animals on Earth live in Kenya. Most live on savannas. Savannas are large grasslands in areas where the weather is hot all year. There are two seasons—a **wet season** and a **dry season**. The animals shown on these pages all live on the savanna in Kenya.

Elephants are the biggest land animals. Some live on savannas, and some live in forests. Read about why elephants are being hunted (on pages 28–29) and how people are helping them.

Weaver birds weave their nests upside down. They live on savannas.

Giraffes are the tallest animals. They feed on the leaves of bushes and trees, especially acacia trees.

Hippopotamuses live in lakes or rivers during the day and come out to feed at night. They eat grasses, leaves, and fruit.

African wild dogs

lion

hyena

jackal

The lion is the national symbol of Kenya. Lions are **carnivores** and **predators**. A carnivore eats other animals, and a predator hunts them. Other savanna carnivores are African wild dogs, hyenas, and jackals.

27

National parks

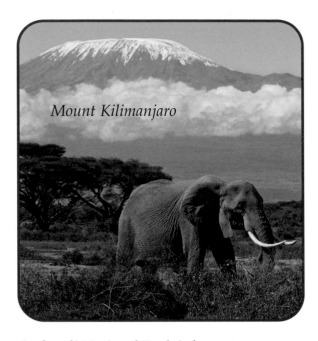

Mount Kilimanjaro

Amboseli National Park is home to many kinds of wild animals. The park also has spectacular views of Mount Kilimanjaro, the highest mountain in Africa.

Many kinds of fish, crabs, sea urchins, sea jellies, and sea stars, like the one above, can be seen in Marine Reserves.

Kenya's elephants and black rhinos are in grave danger from **poachers**. Poachers are illegal hunters who kill animals for their body parts, such as elephant tusks and rhino horns. Elephant tusks are taken for their **ivory**, a hard white material from which many kinds of objects are made. Rhino horns are ground into medicines.

National Parks and Reserves

To help save its wildlife, Kenya has set up protected areas called **National Parks** or **National Reserves**. Some of these protected areas are on land. The ones in or beside oceans are called Marine Parks or Marine Reserves. Some national parks have animal orphanages, which take care of baby animals whose families have been killed by poachers.

This baby black rhino is being fed milk at Nairobi National Park. Its mother has been killed by poachers. There are very few black rhinos left.

Injured animals such as this cheetah are cared for at the Nairobi Park. They need to be held by people many hours each day.

This picture shows elephant tusks that were seized from poachers. People use the tusks to make religious objects or works of art.

The David Sheldrick Wildlife Trust is near Amboseli National Park. It takes in young elephants whose mothers have been hunted for their tusks. When the calves are brought to the shelter, they are often very sad and need someone to be with them night and day. Staff members feed them milk from bottles and often sleep near them.

Kenya safari

Many visitors come to Kenya to experience a **safari**. On a safari, travelers can see and photograph animals such as elephants, lions, and wildebeest in their natural habitats. The Maasai Mara Game Reserve is a popular safari park, but some people enjoy being near the ocean. Their "safaris" may include snorkels and bathing suits!

The Maasai Mara National Reserve is a large game reserve in southwestern Kenya. Each year, more than a million wildebeest cross the Mara River inside the park to find fresh grasses and drinking water on the other side. Many tourists travel to this park to watch this exciting show of nature. Crocodiles hiding in the river make this crossing very dangerous for the wildebeest.

Tourists travel in small buses and trucks over the open savanna. Animals, like this giraffe, can be seen up close. There are camps and lodges where people can stay overnight.

Mombasa Marine National Park and Reserve is in the Indian Ocean on Kenya's coast. It is a popular snorkeling and diving location with many coral reefs. This sea slug lives in a coral reef in the waters of the Mombasa Reserve.

At several parks, Maasai men welcome tourists with their traditional jumping dance.

31

Glossary

Note: Some boldfaced words are defined where they appear in the book.

border An imaginary line that separates countries or areas of land

canyon A deep valley with steep sides

carnivore An animal that eats other animals

coast Land that is beside an ocean

colony An area ruled by a country that is far away

coral polyp A tiny ocean animal with a soft round body and tentacles around its mouth

coral reef An area of an ocean that is made up of live coral polyps and dead corals

dry season A time of year when very little or no rain falls

equator An imaginary line around the center of Earth

lava Magma, or liquid rock, which has erupted out of a volcano

mangrove A tropical tree with large roots that grows in swamps along the coast

nomadic Describing people who do not settle in one place but constantly move from one location to another

predator An animal that hunts and eats other animals

refugee A person forced to leave his or her country because of a war or natural disaster

savanna A broad, grassy plain that is often treeless and is located in tropical areas

settler A person who makes a new home in a place where few other people live

tropical Describing areas with hot climates found near the equator

volcano An opening in Earth's crust where hot lava, gases, ash, and rocks shoot out

wet season A time of year when an area receives most of its rainfall for the year

Index